The Runaway Beignet

By Connie Collins Morgan

Illustrated by Herb Leonhard

PELICAN PUBLISHING COMPANY

GRETNA 2014

To my grandmother, Marie Landry Menard, who graced this life for 103 years, and to my mother, Bernice Menard Collins, who at 88 years still embodies the essence of joie de vivre.—C. C. M.

For Bill Watterson—H. L.

A special thanks to Rachel Morgan, who helped write the beignet's rhythmic refrain.

The word "Pelican" and the depiction of a pelican are trademarks of Pelican Publishing Company, Inc., and are registered in the U.S. Patent and Trademark Office.

Library of Congress Cataloging-in-Publication Data

Morgan, Connie Collins.
  The runaway beignet / by Connie Collins Morgan ; illustrated by Herb Leonhard.
       pages cm
  Summary: In this version of "The Gingerbread Man," a lonely baker's freshly fried beignet comes to life and dashes through the sights of New Orleans's French Quarter to escape being eaten.
  ISBN 978-1-4556-1912-2 (hardcover : alk. paper) — ISBN 978-1-4556-1913-9 (e-book) [1. Folklore.] I. Leonhard, Herb, illustrator. II. Title.
  PZ8.1.M822Ru 2014
  398.2—dc23
  [E]

201303045

Printed in Malaysia

Published by Pelican Publishing Company, Inc.
1000 Burmaster Street, Gretna, Louisiana 70053

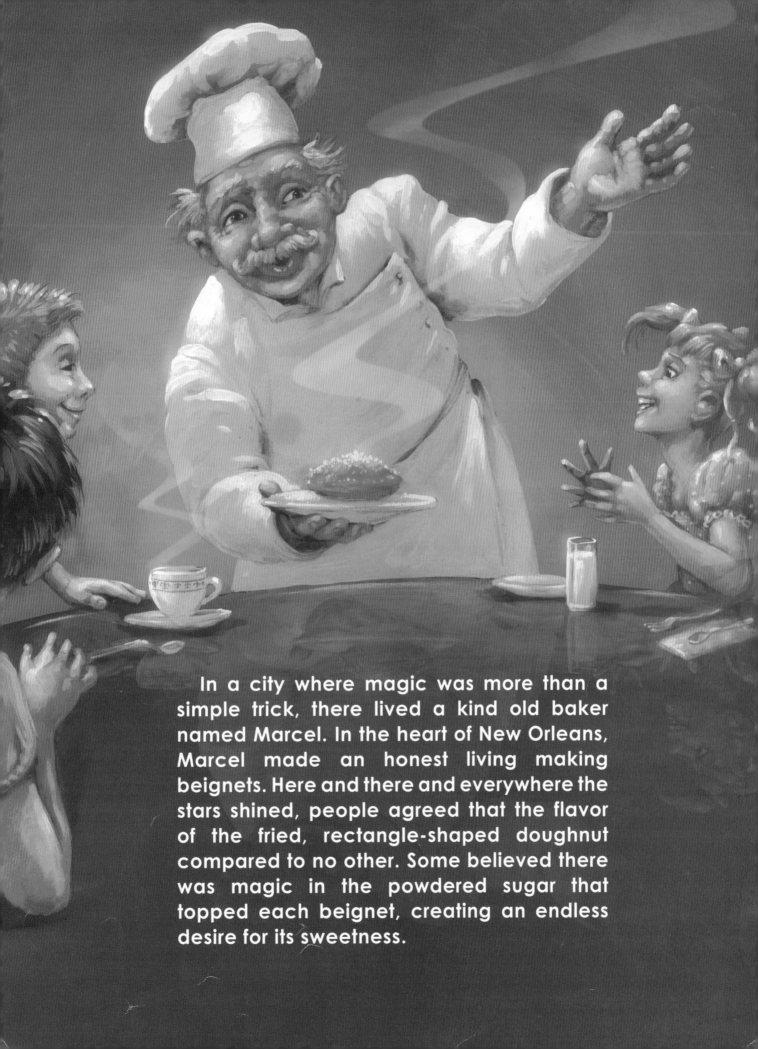

In a city where magic was more than a simple trick, there lived a kind old baker named Marcel. In the heart of New Orleans, Marcel made an honest living making beignets. Here and there and everywhere the stars shined, people agreed that the flavor of the fried, rectangle-shaped doughnut compared to no other. Some believed there was magic in the powdered sugar that topped each beignet, creating an endless desire for its sweetness.

Many people thought that the baker could have been rich had he not given his pastries to the poor. He even wandered the cobblestone streets feeding beignets to hungry pigeons. Sadly enough, the baker had no family, and even though hundreds of people visited his shop day after day, Marcel was lonely.

One morning, a weary stranger wearing a gray coat, colorful scarf, and red shoes entered the shop. "May I please have a glass of cool water?" he asked.

Marcel gave the stranger water and a bag of fresh beignets. "Take this with you. *Bon appétit.*"

"But I have no money to pay you," said the stranger.

Marcel smiled. "I'm not asking for any money."

"Your generosity surpasses the fine aroma of your beignets," said the stranger. "Take this bag of sugar. When the sun welcomes the day, sprinkle it on the first beignet you cook and wish for anything you want."

"I've never heard of anything like this!" Marcel mumbled, reaching for a water pitcher behind him. When he turned around to refill the stranger's glass, he was gone.

Early the next morning, Marcel opened the bag of sugar. "I must have lost my mind to believe that man." He put two dots of sugar on top of the first-cooked beignet. "*Mais*, that looks like two little eyes," he said, laughing. He added a nose and a smiling mouth. "That face makes you look like a beignet boy!" As the sugar melted into the pastry, Marcel remembered the words of the stranger and whispered, "I wish that you were a real boy."

To Marcel's surprise, the beignet boy blinked his eyes and jumped upon the table.

"*Aiyee, look at me!*"

Marcel's eyes lit up. "*Bon dieu,* the beignet boy is alive!" But when Marcel reached for the beignet boy, he jumped to the floor.

"Hee, hee, hee—you can't catch me!" And he dashed out the door.

Marcel ran down the street shouting,

"Stop!

Come back! Mon petit garçon!"

But the beignet boy just smiled as he sang,
"Believe you me,
I'm gonna get away!
You not gonna taste
this little beignet!"

Down Canal Street and through the French Quarter he zipped. Running across a bandstand of jazz players, the beignet boy leaped upon a drum with a burst of powdered sugar.

"Aiyee, look at me!" he sang, shaking his little beignet hips. The crowd stomped and romped to the rhythm of "When the Saints Go Marching In."

Suddenly, the drummer sniffed the aroma of the freshly fried beignet. "Hey, wassup?"

The beignet boy yelled, "Oh no—end of show!" He dashed off the bandstand singing,
"Believe you me,
I'm gonna get away!
You not gonna taste
this little beignet!"
"Stop! Come back!" shouted the jazz players. But the beignet boy kept running.

When he came to Jackson Square, the beignet boy posed in disguise while a street artist painted his picture. Marcel and the jazz players ran around and around Jackson Square. "Hee, hee, hee—they don't see me!"

All of a sudden, the street artist whiffed the sweet beignet aroma. "Mm, you come wiz me, no?"

"No!" said the beignet boy, racing out of Jackson Square.

"Stop! Come back!" the artist yelled, "Zee beignet does not run away from zee André!"

The beignet boy dashed along the Mississippi River past a mime, around a juggler, and between the stilts of a street performer. His song echoed throughout the Riverwalk.

"Believe you me,
I'm gonna get away!
You not gonna taste
this little beignet!"

Marcel, the jazz players, and André, the zany artist, followed the beignet boy into the French Market. Their reckless chase upset the merchants selling their wares. Fleeing the scene, the beignet boy zipped out of the market wearing a Mardi Gras mask and colorful beads.

"Aiyee, look at me!"

Marcel spun out of the market wearing a lady's dress. The jazz players rolled out in their underwear. The artist stumbled out with a crawfish on his head!

Even the upset merchants were lured by the sweet aroma and joined the chase.

"Stop! Come back!" they all cried. But the beignet boy rushed away, singing,

"Believe you me,
I'm gonna get away!
You not gonna taste
this little beignet!"

The beignet boy ran alongside a mule-drawn carriage. When he leaped on the back of the mule, it galloped away. "Hee, hee, hee—I'm finally free!" said the beignet boy, sitting snugly on the mule's back.

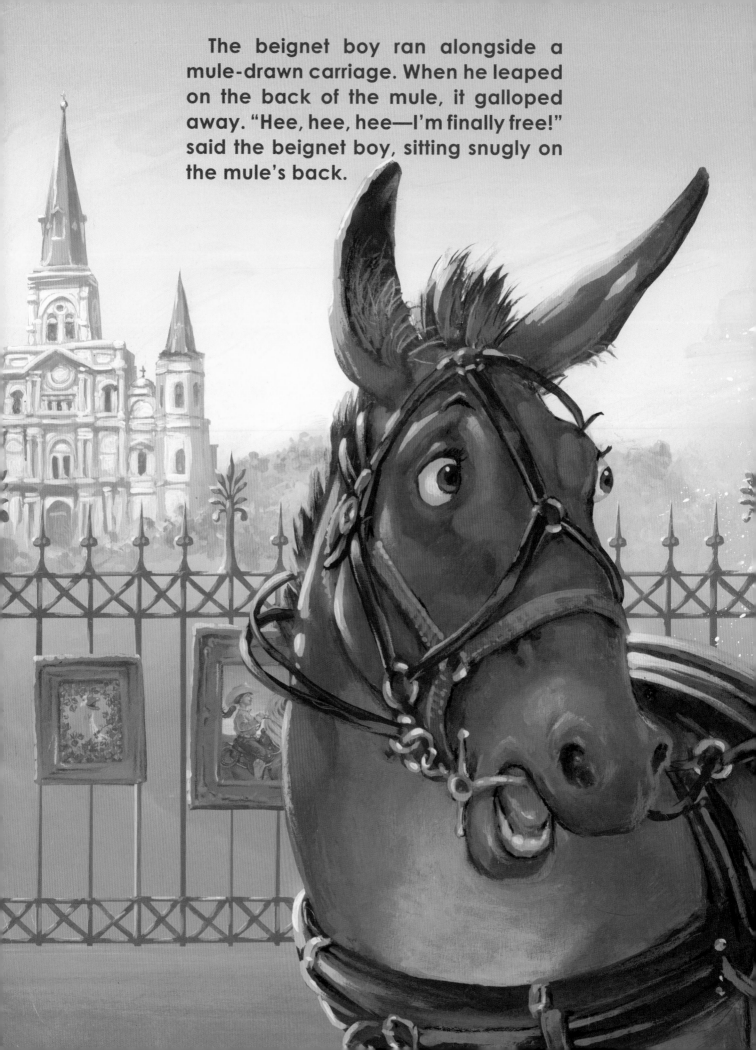

"Oh no," Marcel cried, "*Mon petit garçon* is gone." So, Marcel, the jazz players, the artist, and all of the merchants trudged back to work.

When the mule finally tired, the beignet boy hid in Jackson Square. A friendly pigeon became his only company. As the sun sank into the stillness of the night and the last sounds of jazz faded into the moonlight, the beignet boy wiped away a tear.

"Believe you me,
I'm glad I got away!
But I wish there were a friend
for this little beignet!"

"I can help you," said the pigeon.
"I know someone who needs a friend."
The pigeon flapped his gray wings and strutted his red feet. As he cocked his head, a band of colorful feathers glistened around his neck.

Suddenly, a whirlwind of pigeons swooped down and lifted the beignet boy into the air.

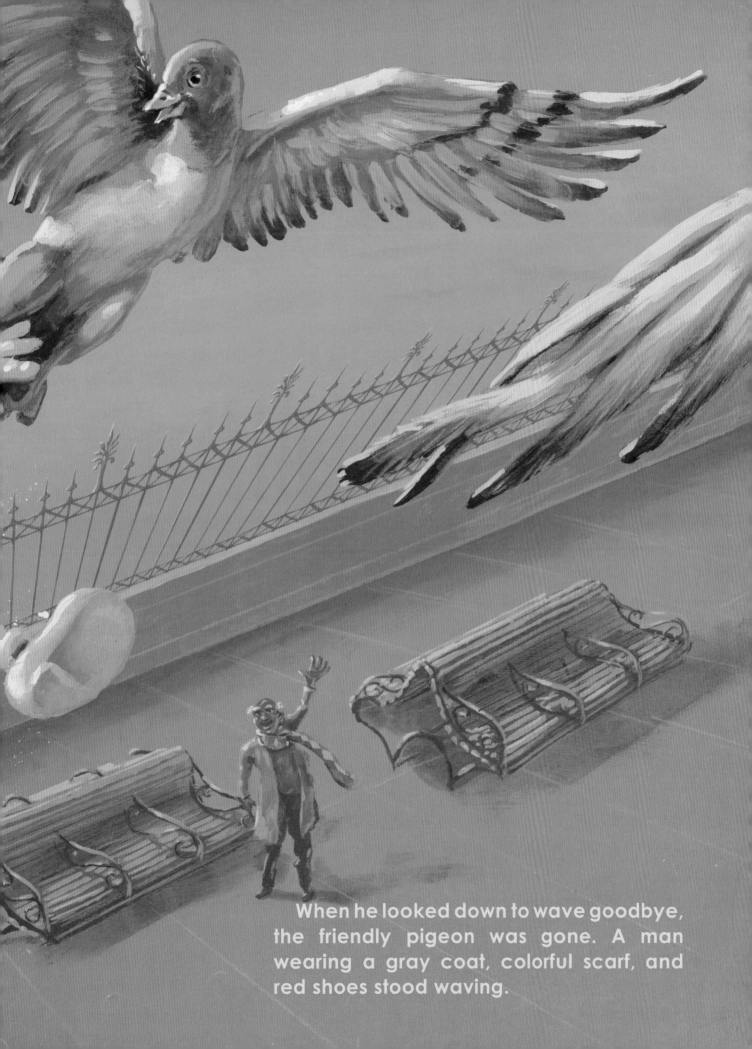

When he looked down to wave goodbye, the friendly pigeon was gone. A man wearing a gray coat, colorful scarf, and red shoes stood waving.

That night, a veil of gray swept across the ground outside of Marcel's shop. When he opened his front door, the pigeons flapped their wings in unison as the beignet boy sang,

"Believe you me,
I'll never run away!
I'm always gonna be
your little beignet!"

Marcel beamed with delight. "You're *mon petit garçon*."

"Hee, hee, hee—I'm as happy as can be!"
said the beignet boy, and he gave Marcel
a big, powdery, beignet kiss!

Children's Folklore

In the timeless world of folklore, children explore the cultural blending of food, music, language, traditions, customs, and practices. These elements promote the originality and distinctiveness of a region, revealing the uniqueness of its people.

The Runaway Beignet celebrates the folklore of New Orleans. The story offers a regional twist to the timeless tale of *The Gingerbread Man*. The beignet's rambunctious romp through the city provides a glimpse of the musical heritage of New Orleans, a city known by many as the birthplace of jazz. Also showcased in the beignet's chase are historical landmarks that remain cornerstones for cultural preservation. The French Quarter, also called the Vieux Carré, the St. Louis Cathedral in Jackson Square, and the French Market are links to the city's past. The dialects spoken by each character give a flavor of the ethnic influences that make New Orleans a cultural melting pot. Woven into the story are costumes worn during the Mardi Gras celebration that represent folk traditions. The main character of the story, a beignet boy, represents an important food tradition. French colonists brought beignets to New Orleans when they left Europe.

Folklore has survived in literature for more than two thousand years. It continues to captivate the imagination of children around the world.

Glossary

Aiyee (ah ē)—A French expression used to express emotion when other words are not available.

Bon Appétit (bōn'-ä-pā-tē)—An expression used to wish someone enjoyment for food he or she is about to eat.

Bon Dieu (bŏn Dū)—A French expression that literally means "good God" but is more often used as "good heavens."

Beignet (bĕn-yā')—A light, square doughnut sprinkled with powdered sugar.

Crawfish—A small freshwater crustacean that resembles a lobster.

Fleur-de-Lis—A type of flower that is used as a symbol. There are three fleur-de-lis on the flag of New Orleans.

French Market—A large, open marketplace similar to a flea market. The French Market merchants sell all kinds of groceries, trinkets, clothes, books, and more.

French Quarter—Also called the Vieux Carré. The oldest neighborhood in the city of New Orleans.

Jackson Square—An open area in the heart of the French Quarter. Inside the square is a statue of Andrew Jackson, hero of the Battle of New Orleans. Jackson became the seventh president of the United States.

King Cake—An oval pastry sprinkled with colored sugar in the Mardi Gras colors of purple, green, and gold. A plastic baby is hidden inside the cake. The person who receives the slice of cake with the baby must buy the king cake for the next party.

Mais (may)—Literally, French for "but." In casual conversation, "yes" or "well, yeah."

Mardi Gras (mahr-dee grah)—Literally, French for "Fat Tuesday." A festival occurring the day before Lent begins, consisting of parades, costumes, and lots of food.

Mon Petit Garçon (mōn pa.ti gär-sō^n)—French for "my little boy."

Riverwalk—A mall located in the Central Business District of New Orleans along the Mississippi River waterfront.

St. Louis Cathedral—The oldest Catholic cathedral having continual services in the United States. It overlooks Jackson Square.

Steamboat Natchez—A steam-powered sternwheeler built in 1975, still in operation on the Mississippi River.